The Divine Salvage

*First Lesson Sermons For Sundays
After Pentecost (Middle Third)
Cycle A*

Curtis and Tempe Fussell

CSS Publishing Company, Inc., Lima, Ohio

THE DIVINE SALVAGE

Copyright © 1998 by
CSS Publishing Company, Inc.
Lima, Ohio

All rights reserved. No part of this publication may be reproduced in any manner whatsoever without the prior permission of the publisher, except in the case of brief quotations embodied in critical articles and reviews. Inquiries should be addressed to: Permissions, CSS Publishing Company, Inc., P.O. Box 4503, Lima, Ohio 45802-4503.

Scripture quotations are from the *Revised Standard Version of the Bible*, copyrighted 1946, 1952 ©, 1971, 1973, by the Division of Christian Education of the National Council of the Churches of Christ in the USA. Used by permission.

Scripture references marked NKJV are from *The New King James Bible—New Testament*. Copyright © 1979, 1982, Thomas Nelson Inc., Publishers.

Library of Congress Cataloging-in-Publication Data

Fussell, R. Curtis, 1953-
 The divine salvage : first lesson sermons for Sundays after Pentecost (middle third), Cycle A / Curtis and Tempe Fussell.
     p. cm.
 Includes bibliographical references.
 ISBN 0-7880-1237-1 (alk. paper)
     1. Presbyterian Church (U.S.A.)—Sermons. 2. Church year sermons. 3. Bible. O.T.—Sermons. 4. Sermons, American. I. Fussell, Tempe, 1954-   . II. Title.
BX9178.A1F87   1998
252'.64—dc21   98-11289
                                                                                                  CIP

This book is available in the following formats, listed by ISBN:
 0-7880-1237-1 Book

PRINTED IN U.S.A.

*To the unassuming ones who have
great significance in our lives:*
*Calee
Hannah
Rachel
Robert*

*and to the saints at our churches:
Marys
Richlands
Thompson Valley
West Fork Chapel*

Table Of Contents

Foreword	7

Proper 12
Pentecost 10
Ordinary Time 17
  Salvaging Our Lives
  Genesis 29:15-28
	9

Proper 13
Pentecost 11
Ordinary Time 18
  The Honor Of A Limp
  Genesis 32:22-31
	15

Proper 14
Pentecost 12
Ordinary Time 19
  The Waste In Comparison
  Genesis 37:1-4, 12-28
	23

Proper 15
Pentecost 13
Ordinary Time 20
  God Sends Us Ahead
  Genesis 45:1-15
	27

Proper 16
Pentecost 14
Ordinary Time 21
  Come Out, Come Out, Wherever You Are!
  Exodus 1:8—2:10
	31

Proper 17   37
Pentecost 15
Ordinary Time 22
    Growing No Feathers
    Exodus 3:1-15

Proper 18   41
Pentecost 16
Ordinary Time 23
    Bloody Doorposts
    Exodus 12:1-14

Proper 19   49
Pentecost 17
Ordinary Time 24
    Going Through The Waters
    Exodus 14:19-31

Proper 20   55
Pentecost 18
Ordinary Time 25
    The Rain Of Bread
    Exodus 16:2-15

Proper 21   61
Pentecost 19
Ordinary Time 26
    It's Not Over When The Fat Lady Sings
    Exodus 17:1-7

Lectionary Preaching After Pentecost   65

Foreword

We are glad that you are joining us in the search for insight and inspiration into preaching from these Old Testament texts. Recent research shows that not many sermons are preached from the First Testament, particularly Genesis and Exodus. In a recent article by Ronald Allen in *Pulpit Digest*, he notes that "today's preachers focus on the Second Testament ... (T)he Gospels have the lion's share of the attention ... The First Testament is the primary text for only 24 percent of the homilies with Isaiah, Jeremiah, and Psalms providing over half of the texts for these sermons."[1] If Allen is correct, then our congregations very seldom hear messages from Genesis and Exodus. The sermons in this book are based on passages in the First Testament that can only be considered "classic" biblical stories with which every believer ought to be familiar. We hope you, as a preacher, will preach on these texts, helping your congregation become familiar with these ancient stories, and to know them as stories that remind us of how God is still powerfully present in our lives today.

The report on preaching to which Allen refers also indicates that contemporary preaching emphasizes the all-forgiving character of God, giving the impression that God is soft and unconcerned with what we believe and what we stand for. Yet among the main characteristics of the First Testament is the demand by God for us to be accountable; to act in ways that exhibit that we are strong in the ways of God and the world, as the people of God. Preaching from the Bible demands that we articulate both the unconditional mercy of God and the unconditional demands of God, that we may become the whole people of God.

In the sermons presented here we have been conscious of God's unconditional mercy and demands. We have been aware of these themes because the texts themselves are conscious of both God's mercy and demands. The God of ancient Israel and the God of Jesus does not merely seek to help us live in a difficult world. More is at stake here than our well-being. Above all, what is primary is the faithfulness of God. Genesis and Exodus seek to flesh this out, that the God of Israel and all of creation is a faithful God. God's faithfulness is not one-sided though. God expects to participate in a partnership of fidelity. In receiving and living in God's faithful promises, our over-arching desire is to bear witness to that trust.

In that light there is throughout these passages a profound testimony to the presence of God in the chaos of life, in the self-serving actions of even chosen people, and in the setbacks and difficulties that inflict life. Within all these dilemmas, these passages seek to reveal God's steadfast love. The result is then not a moral or psychological lesson, but the responsive human act to remember, to honor, to glorify and worship the faithful God of Israel. The "Larger Catechism" of the "Westminster Confession of Faith" puts it succinctly when its first statement declares that our "chief and highest end is to glorify God, and fully to enjoy Him forever." To glorify God and to live in and know the joy of God is the thrust of these biblical passages. To the end that we have pointed in that direction and upheld this theme in these sermons, we will have fulfilled our calling as ministers of the Word of God.

---

1. Ronald Allen, "What We Are Really Preaching: A Report on Empirical Studies of Preaching," in *Pulpit Digest*, September/October 1997, Vol. LXXVIII, No. 5 (Inver Grove Heights, Minn.: Logos Publications), p. 80.

Proper 12 • *Pentecost 10* • *Ordinary Time 17*

Salvaging Our Lives

Genesis 29:15-28

If you have ever made an in-depth investigation of your family history, a genealogy, then you probably came across some ancestors who would qualify as so-called "black sheep of the family." Among my own ancestors my father came across a family will dating back to shortly before the Civil War. In that will it speaks of my great-great-great-grandmother selling off slaves. In fact, the will indicates that the slave family she owned was to be divided up at her death. When I first heard about this I was shocked and horrified. I could not believe it was true until I read the will myself. To tell you now in public this bit of family history is very distressing for me. It's not merely embarrassing; it is shameful to me; and yet, it is a fact of my ancestral history that I cannot erase and must acknowledge.

One of the most amazing things about the Hebrew Scriptures, the Old Testament, is its willingness to describe the ancestors of Israel in all their less than flattering human actions and traits. The Jews have had the courage and wisdom not to hide our human nature, but to reveal it in all its forms, from the most splendid to the most vile. We have only to think of David and how he is portrayed as one who follows after God's own heart, and yet this same David is one who falls to adultery and murder. Scripture hangs the family clothing out on the line for everyone to see.

Here in this passage we read about an employment deal worked out between Jacob and Laban, who is Jacob's uncle on his mother's side. The occasion for this deal is the old story line of "boy meets girl and falls in love." Jacob had met Rachel, Laban's daughter, and learned that she was related to him. How fortunate for Jacob because it apparently was love at first sight. How fortunate also for Jacob because the custom of that day encouraged the marrying of distant relatives. We are even told that on that first meeting, he was so moved by Rachel that "Jacob kissed Rachel, and wept aloud" (29:11). No doubt it was a weeping with joy. Such a bold gesture declares to us how Jacob was utterly bowled over and swept off his feet by Rachel. Matters could not have been more fortuitous for Jacob. Everything seems to work in his favor.

But unpleasant surprises have a way of entering even the most fortunate lives of people. Enter now Rachel's father Laban. If you remember how Jacob came to Haran where Laban lives, then you will remember that Jacob had stolen the blessing that by right belonged to his brother Esau as the firstborn son. By deception, trickery, and shameless lying, Jacob fooled his father Isaac into giving him the firstborn blessing. When Esau discovered what had happened, he vowed to kill Jacob. And so to save his life, Jacob's mother Rebekah sends him far off to Laban's home at Haran, in what is today northern Iraq. But in the person of Laban Jacob meets someone who is as good at trickery and deception as Jacob himself. The deal with Laban was for Jacob to work seven years, after which he could marry Rachel.

And so Jacob worked seven years and it was time for the wedding. There was a great wedding festival and Jacob thought he had married Rachel. But in the morning he discovered that he had not spent his wedding night with Rachel, but instead with Leah, her older sister. How Jacob did not know he had married Leah and how he did not know he had spent the night with Leah is not told. Maybe there was too much make-up and wedding gown, maybe too much drinking, maybe exhaustion from greeting too many guests. It seems unbelievable, but however it happened, it happened. But it tells us that Jacob trusted Laban, much as Esau probably trusted his brother Jacob. When Jacob discovered the trickery, he immediately charged Laban and demanded, "What is this you have done to me?"

Here now we find a moral lesson: That which goes round comes around. Esau could just as well have spoken these words when

Jacob deceived his father Isaac and stole his birthright blessing: "What is this you have done to me?" Now it is Jacob's turn to suffer the humiliation and pain of being deceived and tricked. Laban then explains to Jacob that Leah had the right to be married first because she was the eldest daughter. The rights and priority of the firstborn are by now well impressed on Jacob.

But all is not lost for Jacob. Laban proposes to Jacob that if he will work for him another seven years, he may marry Rachel in seven days. And so Jacob agrees, and in seven days he marries Rachel, the love of his life. But all this is a sordid affair. Laban uses and abuses Jacob to achieve his own ends. And while it may be said that Jacob gets only what he has given, it is still another sad story of deception in which people are used and hurt. Of particular note is the treatment of Leah and Rachel, who seem to be played as mere objects in Laban's hand even though they are his daughters. What is absent is a sense of decency and honesty.

But there is something else absent here that is striking. I don't know if you noticed it or not, but throughout this entire drama not one word is mentioned about God. Apparently, God has no role in what takes place between Jacob, Laban, Rachel, and Leah. The only power that seems to be at work here is the power of deception and the power of custom. One begins to wonder, "Where is God in all this?"

Well, perhaps God is at work at bringing about a sense of justice in regard to Esau. The deceiver Jacob has met another capable deceiver and been duped. Perhaps the memory and telling of this story was a way of reminding people that our sins come back to haunt us. But there is no hint in this story that it carries such a moral message. On the contrary, after his marriage to Leah and Rachel, Jacob is soon blessed with eleven children who become the figureheads for the eleven tribes of Israel. In a real sense, it is the birth of a nation! Leah, in fact, gives birth to six of these children! So Laban's deception becomes a blessing in disguise. God is indeed present with Jacob, making him wealthy in children so that the promise to Abraham will be fulfilled through him, that his descendants would be as numerous as the stars in the heavens (Genesis 22:17).

There is a striking similarity here with what we find in the New Testament when Joseph's betrothal to Mary is marred by what appears to be a devious action. Mary is found to be pregnant before she and Joseph are married, so that Joseph decides quietly to break off the engagement. Joseph might well have said to Mary the very words Jacob spoke to Laban: "What is this you have done to me?" But again what appears to be a misdeed proves to be blessing. Of course, in the story about the birth of Jesus, God speaks directly to Mary and Joseph, unlike the story of Jacob and Laban.

In the story of Jacob and Laban, where God is neither seen nor heard directly, we find in many ways our own story. Is it not true that we ourselves live lives in which God does not directly speak to us? And yet, as believers we affirm that God is with us, working, as we say, "in mysterious ways" to achieve some good. With the eyes of faith we can perceive the hand of God moving through our lives to make us victorious and not victims.

The apostle Paul makes this affirmation himself in the face of many hardships during his missionary work when he says, "In everything God works for good with those who love him" (Romans 8:28). It is important though to make clear that Paul does not propose a "Pollyanna" perspective by this statement, as though if you are on God's side, then nothing but good things will happen to you. If anyone provides a testimony against such a silly, naive perspective, it is Paul. Because of his preaching ministry, Paul suffered imprisonment and countless beatings and often was brought near to death. He received 39 lashes on five occasions, three times he was beaten with rods, on one occasion he was stoned, he was shipwrecked three times, and he had to endure hunger, hardship, toil, and fear from every corner (2 Corinthians 11:23-28). And yet Paul can proclaim, "We know that in everything God works for good with those who love him, who are called according to his purpose" (Romans 8:28).

As Jacob experienced abuse at the hands of Laban, we too may suffer times when other people use and abuse us, times when people take advantage of us, lead us astray with deception and humiliate us. Sometimes we even use and abuse ourselves, thinking that if we had taken this action or that action, then life would have turned out better. We all go through trials and tribulations in life, sometimes by the hands of others and sometimes by our own hands. But blessed are those who learn from their mistakes. And blessed are those who have the eyes to see and the ears to hear the presence of God in their lives. For God salvages our lives and makes something good out of them. We do not have to be victims. On the contrary, we can through God choose to be victorious.

In Chicago in 1927, Buckminster Fuller had reached the depths of despair. He was already deeply depressed over the death of his little daughter, Alexandra, when he was fired from his job without severance pay. His self-confidence was shattered in the face of these events. He felt that life had turned against him. He was sure his wife and second daughter, Allegra, would be much better off if he weren't around. In his despair he began drinking heavily, and one night walked down to the shore of Lake Michigan with the intention of throwing himself in to drown. But as the chilly wind sharpened his senses and he watched the waves crashing on the shore, he began to think about his situation more closely.

The exquisite design and order of the beach reminded him of God. His next insight was that God had given him some unique experiences that could, if shared with others, be of benefit to them. He resolved at that moment to share his experiences with others and not worry about making a living. Buckminster reasoned: if God really has use of me, then He will not allow my family to starve; He will see to it that my resolve is carried out.

Buckminster Fuller went on to make that small resolve into a large achievement. He became one of the most famous men in the world, being introduced at speaking engagements as "poet, prophet, mathematician, philosopher, scientist, architect, and inventor of the geodesic dome."[1]

Buckminster will tell you that God salvaged his life that night by the shore of Lake Michigan. Buckminster could have wallowed in self-pity and blamed others for mistreating him, including God. But he didn't! He resolved *not* to be a victim, but instead through God to be victorious.

At the end of the Book of Genesis, Joseph, the son of Jacob, tells his brothers, "You meant evil against me; but God meant it for good" (Genesis 50:20). It could well be that Joseph learned those words from his father Jacob. After all, no one better experienced these words than Jacob. There are two ways to approach life. You can go through life blaming others for life's setbacks and wallow in self-pity and consider yourself a victim. Or, you can resolve to press on forward in the face of misfortune, knowing that God goes with you and will make you victorious in the end. It will take courage and determination to do this, but in time those with eyes of faith will surely say, "God was with me all the way. It was not always obvious, but I see now that God was with me."

Curtis Fussell

---

1. Adapted from King Duncan's sermon, "There Is A War Going On," in *Preaching for Lent and Easter* (Knoxville, Tenn.: Seven Worlds, 1988), disk, PLE7.

Proper 13 • Pentecost 11 • Ordinary Time 18

The Honor Of A Limp

Genesis 32:22-31

Richard Sears was a young man when his father died, and so he had to go to work to support the family. He took a job on the railroad and worked his way up to station agent in North Redwood, Minnesota. To earn extra money he sold coal and lumber. One day a box full of watches was delivered to his station by mistake. The local jeweler decided he didn't want the watches. But instead of sending the watches back to the company, Richard Sears decided to buy the watches himself and proceeded to sell them. In a short time he made a nice profit. Richard Sears' actions became the first step in founding what would later be called the "Sears, Roebuck Company."[1]

We all love such "rags to riches" stories. The determination and persistence in these stories are like true fairy tales. They end with "and they lived happily ever after." The appeal of such stories, I think, lies in their ability to inspire us. They inspire us to focus our physical, mental, and spiritual powers. Such stories are models telling us that we too can succeed against difficult obstacles. Such stories tell us that we do not have to be born with a silver spoon in our mouths to be successful. Rags to riches stories are stories full of the wisdom of the world: that hard work, persistence, and determination do indeed have a reward.

The story of Jacob is also a rags to riches story. Only this story has an added twist: Jacob is born into a family that is chosen by God and so we assume he is blessed from the start. But in the story of Jacob it is clear his success also involves struggling to be chosen and blessed.[2] The story of Jacob is a powerful story, telling us that while life is indeed a gift from God, we still must struggle and wrestle with life to be blessed by God. It is a story very much in line with Jesus' remark that "to whom much is given, of him much is required" (Luke 12:48). In the case of Jacob, life is given to him as an heir to God's promise to Abraham and life is also grasped by him; hence the name Jacob, which in Hebrew means "heel grabber" or "overreacher." The story of Jacob is the story of struggle in life before God, who both blesses us and gives us the space to make our lives blessed. This is the character of Jacob. And the passage before us gives him credit for being a person who knows how to act in ways that ensure the blessings of life and God.

Our story begins many years earlier when Jacob had stolen Esau's birthright. This birthright was a blessing from their father Isaac which rightfully belonged to Esau as the firstborn son. In stealing this blessing it gave Jacob, rather than Esau, the right to inherit the leadership of the tribe when their father Isaac died. When Esau discovers this theft, he vows in vengeance to kill Jacob. And so Jacob flees from Canaan, the land promised to Abraham and his descendants, and goes far away to northern Mesopotamia, modern-day Iraq, to live with relatives.

After many years, the time has now come for Jacob to return to his homeland. On his way back Jacob sends a messenger to Esau telling him of his return home. The messenger then returns to tell Jacob, "Esau is coming to meet you and 400 men are with him!" To Jacob this can only mean one thing: Esau is coming to carry out his vow of vengeance to kill him.

With this threat, Jacob again acts with cunning, or perhaps better to say, with wisdom. First, he divides his people into two camps to ensure that at least half of his people will escape if Esau attacks. Second, he prays to God for deliverance from Esau. And third, he lavishly sends wonderful gifts to Esau in the hope that it will quiet his anger and remind him that they are brothers. We find Jacob doing all he can to ensure that Esau will not carry out his vow of vengeance.

After making these thorough defenses, Jacob is now alone at the Jabbok River crossing on the evening before Esau is due to arrive. Suddenly, we are told that "a man wrestled with him until the break of day." Who this "man" is, is not entirely clear. He is described at various times as a "man," as an "angel," and as "God." Who this being is, is not clear, but such is the nature of God. All we can say in the end is what Jacob himself relates: that he has seen the "face of God" and so he called the place "Peniel," which means in Hebrew "the face of God."

But why has God come to wrestle with Jacob? Jacob is under threat from Esau. Why does God attack Jacob? Why doesn't God attack Esau to protect Jacob who has been given the blessing? Could it be that God attacks Jacob because Jacob deserves a reprimand for his deceitful, immoral actions against Esau? Or perhaps this attack isn't real at all; just a psychological struggle of guilt in Jacob's heart and mind for stealing Esau's birthright. And yet in fact, there is nothing in this passage, nor anywhere else in the Bible, that says God is angry about Jacob's deception of Esau. And there is nothing in this passage that says Jacob felt remorse and seeks repentance on account of what he did to Esau.

Others point out that Jacob was morally and spiritually lacking. They describe Jacob as one who has acted in a "thoroughly self-centered and self-serving" way all his life. His efforts make him "successful," but he's "faithless."[3] So God attacks Jacob and leaves him limping to reveal that God has redeemed Jacob from his past immoral behavior. But we also see that when Jacob demands a blessing, his struggle with God only becomes another example that he has "remained the one who grabs."[4] Only by God's grace is Jacob, the cunning, self-serving scoundrel, allowed to walk away from the wrestling match with only a limp.

No doubt we can describe Jacob as a scoundrel who is self-serving and self-centered, but if we do I think we run the risk of denying much that is true about our own lives. We may in fact be in danger of rejecting Jesus' demand to "strive to enter by the narrow door" (Luke 13:24). The point here is that striving for the good gifts of God is indeed a proper witness to the grace of God. The apostle Paul highlights this witness in saying, "I press on to make it my own, because Christ Jesus has made me his own" (Philippians 3:12). Paul is determined to take hold of the blessings of Jesus Christ that are given to him, and that is a proper discipleship.

The story of Jacob is a story of struggle, of one who takes hold of God's blessings. Jacob is born into struggle, his life is filled with struggle, some of it of course is brought on by his own actions, and some of it is brought on by the actions of others. But throughout we are aware that Jacob is one who seeks to take hold of God's blessings. Jacob reminds us of this truth: life is full of struggle, even for the blessings of God. In Jacob we see a model of one who asserts himself in a world full of danger. In Jesus' words, he lives as "wise as serpents" (Matthew 10:16), and as one who has a chance to make a difference and receive the blessings of God.

It is important to give Jacob credit for being an example of someone who reaches for life. Jacob does not live a timid, self-deprecating life. On the contrary, here is someone who lives a life worthy of someone who is chosen by God to make a difference in the world. Jacob knows his life is worth something. He knows that what he does and says matters in a significant way, both for himself and for those to whom he is accountable.

William Muehl, a professor of ethics at Yale Divinity School, tells this story about the importance of our lives. "One December afternoon many years ago a group of parents stood in the lobby of a nursery school, waiting to pick up their children after the last pre-Christmas session. As the youngsters ran from their lockers, each one carried in his or her hands the surprise, the brightly wrapped package on which the class had been working for weeks.

"One small boy, trying to run, put on his coat, and wave to his parents all at the same time, slipped and fell. The surprise flew from his grasp and landed on the tile floor with an obvious ceramic crash.

"The child's first reaction was one of stunned silence. But then he set up an inconsolable wail. His father, thinking to minimize the incident and comfort the boy, patted his head and murmured, 'Now that's all right. It really doesn't matter, son. It doesn't matter at all.'

"But the child's mother, somewhat wiser in such situations, dropped to her knees on the floor, swept the boy into her arms and said, 'Oh, but it does matter. It matters a great deal.' And she wept with her son."[5]

Professor Muehl makes the point that God does not dismiss our lives with a pat on the head and a murmured assurance that our lives do not really matter. On the contrary, God gives us this life that we might indeed make something of it. Our lives do matter. Life is worth striving for if the struggle is aimed at the gifts of God. The life we live does make a difference in the world when it is a life lived under the grace of God. The decisions we make, the actions we take, have cosmic significance when they are undertaken before God. And so we are called by God to live strong, decisive lives before God and others.

Jacob is a prime example of this strength we are to display. He reminds us that bold actions do make a difference before God and others. We can live bold lives that are a blessing, or we can live timid lives that don't matter. I am reminded of something the German theologian Martin Luther once said, "Sin boldly and experience the grace of Christ more fully." Luther is not advocating that we commit sins. But he is advocating that we live before God and others with power and strength; not afraid of God but knowing that God expects us to wrestle with Him and the world. What we see in Jacob is one who is honored for his determination and wisdom to act boldly and decisively in a world that is dangerous. Here is someone who teaches us the struggle to lay hold of the things of God. Jacob settled for nothing less than the fullness of life before God.

Jacob's change in name, to being called "Israel," is given as a kind of badge of honor which recognizes his willingness to struggle and lay hold of the things of God. The divine wrestler announces: "Your name shall no longer be called Jacob, but Israel; for you have struggled with God and with men, and have prevailed" (Genesis 32:28 NKJV). Jacob has been given a new name because he has shown strength and endurance in his relationship with God and Esau and Laban. The name "Israel" reminds us that Jacob was chosen, and yet he asserted his chosenness before God and others. Because he was assertive Jacob received a blessing. We know his boldness through these words from Jesus: "Ask, and it will be given to you; seek, and you will find; knock, and it will be opened to you" (Luke 11:9; Matthew 7:7).

One of the more recognized expressions of wisdom in this century came from a psychiatrist named M. Scott Peck. In his book *The Road Less Traveled*, the first three printed words are these: "Life is difficult." Peck goes on to say that a quality life, a life that makes a difference, a life that has significance, demands personal sacrifice, the acceptance of responsibility, and a determined will. It is indeed a "road less traveled." Our story of Jacob at the Jabbok River provides a similar piece of advice: life is difficult and it is not generous to those who are timid and undetermined. Jacob, wrestling for a blessing from God, holds his own, stands firm, and makes demands of God, and God blesses him. No doubt such an example in the Bible is uncommon. Yet Jesus said, "Will God not vindicate his elect, who cry to him day and night? Will he delay long over them? I tell you, he will vindicate them speedily. Nevertheless, when the Son of man comes, will he find faith on earth?" (Luke 18:7-8).

Sometimes this is what faith comes down to, just hanging on, digging in. Isn't this how it has been in your life? You've had times when you were ready to throw in the towel, but you didn't. You hung on, determined to make it through, to make something of your life. You just hung on by your fingernails because that's what life demands, that's what God demands. Winston Churchill gave a commencement address during the height of World War II. That big barrel of a man stood up and repeated only one message: "Never, never, never, never, never. Do not give up. Do not ever give up. Never give up." And then he sat down, and that was it. But people remembered what he said. Why did it strike such a note in the minds of the people? Because that's what life demands, that's the way life has to be lived, and we know that God approves this kind of determination, honors it, and blesses it.[7]

Fred Craddock, a professor of preaching at Emory University, tells how he went to preach at a rural church when he was in seminary. He came into the sanctuary and there hanging on the wall behind the pulpit was a picture. It was a picture of a white English bulldog. A child had brought it from home for Sunday School and had written under it, "Get a bulldog grip on your faith." For weeks he preached under that picture and doubts that those poor, farming people remember anything he said from the pulpit. But he's convinced they do remember that picture and its message. For people struggling to make ends meet, struggling against the world, struggling to see God in their lives, this is what it comes down to: "Get a bulldog grip on your faith."[8] It doesn't matter who you are, your station in life, or how high the steeple is. It comes down to this: Hold on, stand firm, don't ever give up. Ask, and it will be given; seek, and you will find; knock, and the door will be opened to you. This is the witness of Jacob at the Jabbok River crossing. And it is a good witness. A witness of faithful determination to strive before God and others.

Curtis Fussell

---

1. King Duncan, "Success," in *Dynamic Illustrations*, July/August/September 1997 (Knoxville, Tenn.: Seven Worlds Corporation).

2. I am indebted to Fredrick C. Holmgren for the exposition of this passage in his article, "Holding Your Own Against God! Genesis 32:22-32 (In the Context of Genesis 31-33)" in *Interpretation: A Journal of Bible and Theology*, Vol. 50, No. 1, Jan. 1990 (Richmond, Va.: Union Theological Seminary), pp. 5-17.

3. Robert Snell, "Genesis 32:22-32" in *Interpretation: A Journal of Bible and Theology*, Vol. 50, No. 3, July 1996 (Richmond, Va.: Union Theological Seminary), p. 279.

4. *Ibid.*

5. William Muehl, *Why Preach? Why Listen?* (Philadelphia, Pa.: Fortress Press, 1986), p. 92.

6. *Emphasis: A Preaching Journal for the Parish Pastor*, Vol. 27, No.1, May-June 1997 (Lima, Oh.: CSS Publishing Co.), p. 34f.

7. I am indebted to Fred Craddock for these insights and the Churchill illustration from a sermon he preached in Atlanta 1995, sponsored by David Howell and Donald Denton, editors of *Lectionary Homiletics*.

8. *Ibid.*

Proper 14 • Pentecost 12 • Ordinary Time 19

The Waste In Comparison

Genesis 37:1-4, 12-28

Grandparents are some of the most well-balanced people on the face of the earth. They have to be. After all, they have to spend the same amount of time with each grandchild. They have to get something for every grandchild on every trip. And, of course, Christmas gifts must at least look like they cost exactly the same. Jacob has a long way to go in mastering that finesse. He picked a favorite wife and he chose a favorite son. Joseph was the special son who got extravagant gifts and extra attention. He got to stay at home when the brothers had to travel with the herd. Perhaps most cutting of all was the awareness that Jacob loved Joseph's mother more than the mothers of the other brothers.

Favoritism is nice until it's publicized. It's nice for the teacher to show you extra help, but it's no fun to be called the "teacher's pet." Joseph was "daddy's boy." Not only that, but he was a tattle-tale and a dreamer of haughty dreams. Put all this together and Joseph was the brother nobody could or would put up with.

The stories of the families of the patriarchs are filled with favoritism. Isaac was favored by his father Abraham over his half brother, Ishmael. Sly and crafty Rebekah favors Jacob over Esau. And now we hear how Jacob favors Joseph over his ten older brothers. It seems to run in the family, this thing for picking favorite children. Yet, comfortable or not, the way the biblical story is told, picking favorites sets the stage and makes possible the continuing enactment of God's faithfulness.

Unfortunately, favoring a child wreaked havoc in the tents of Abraham, Isaac, and Jacob! Curiously, in every case picking favorites resulted in someone being sent into exile. In the case of Joseph, there was no doubt who had to go. Either Joseph went or Reuben, Simeon, Levi, Judah, Issachar, Zebulun, Gad, Asher, Dan, and Naphtali went. Logistically it made much better sense for Joseph to go. His brothers did not know how to live with favoritism.

It began with a sense of unfairness that led to the men giving "daddy's boy" the silent treatment. Since they were not talking with Joseph there was no vent for their anger. Anger then fermented into raw jealousy. Jealousy looked for the advantage in every weak moment. Every circumstance became an opportunity for revenge. When they saw a pit, "Hey, it's a place to throw our brother!" When they saw a caravan, "Hey, there's some people to buy our brother!" When this opportunity became available they all agreed it was the most fitting: to reduce the prince of the family into the slave of foreigners.

Giving in to jealousy cost the brothers dearly. Booker T. Washington remembered the cost to those who were committed to slavery when he wrote, "You can't hold a man down without staying down with him."

There is a fable retold by William White of the violent potential of jealousy.[1] Two merchants judged their success by comparing their profits. Their rivalry grew each year. God sent an angel to one of the merchants, telling that merchant that God had chosen him for a great gift. "Whatever you desire you will receive," the divine messenger promised. He could have wealth, health, whatever. There was a catch, however. This gift was a lesson from God, because whatever the merchant chose, his competitor would receive twice as much. Ask for power, his competitor would become twice as powerful. "Anything?" the man asked slyly. The angel nodded. And his wish was this, "I ask that you strike me blind in one eye." What a waste. How many of us judge our worth by comparing ourselves or our possessions with others? How many ministers find themselves in competition with other ministers?

There are many instances of the utter waste of jealousy. The most tragic waste of life is recorded in all four gospels. Great men killed the son of God because they were jealous of his authority.

On the occasion of division within the church, Cyprian, then Bishop of Carthage, wrote this of the power of jealousy:

> *But what a gnawing worm of the soul is it, what a plague-spot of our thoughts, what a rust of the heart, to be jealous of another, either in respect of his virtue or of his happiness; that is ... to make other people's glory one's own penalty ... such ... are ever sighing, and groaning, and grieving; and since envy is never put off by the envious, the possessed heart is rent without intermission day and night. Other ills have their limit; and whatever wrong is done, is bounded by the completion of the crime ... Jealousy has no limit; it is an evil continually enduring, and a sin without end.*[2]

For the brothers, Joseph's glory was their penalty. And the tragedy of it all is that no one intervened; no one could intervene. Why didn't Jacob wake up and see where his love for Joseph was leading? Why didn't Reuben take his role as elder brother seriously and speak up more courageously? Perhaps it would have made no difference. We, too, get stuck in our jealousy just as tightly. Sometimes all the well-meaning people in our lives can't make a dent in our desire to be jealous. And it is such a waste.

Judah would be powerful, the lion of all tribes. Zebulun would claim all the lands along the coast. Asher's people would produce rich and luscious foods. Every son of Jacob would have children, forming the twelve tribes of Yahweh.

It is such a waste considering how much time we throw away while we ferment jealousy. Haven't you experienced the temptation of jealousy to pout, to spy, even to commit sabotage? And it all begins by looking aside. Jealousy dwells on other people's gifts, money, fame ... Jealousy sticks my fingers in my ears so that I cannot hear God's purpose for me.

A friend recently told me of a frustrating trip she made to visit an aunt who had just moved into a nursing home. She had hoped to stay several days in the town where her aunt now lived, the two of them seeing the sights, trying the restaurants. And so my friend began a restful journey, stopping when she wanted, seeing the sights along the way. She took in all the parks, several quaint eating places, a couple of outlet malls before arriving in her aunt's town. After settling into the hotel she was dismayed to realize she had already exceeded her budget before she ever got to see her aunt. She had to cut her visit short because she had turned off the road too many times before she ever arrived.

Joseph's brothers also turned aside too often. They were stuck in their jealous distraction. They were too mesmerized by Joseph's good fortune to recognize the fullness of their own lives. Tragically, no one could make the leaders of the tribes of Israel consider their own worth. But there is hope for you and me who remember this story of jealousy and rivalry. Only you and I can keep our joy focused on the important purpose that God has given to us.

Tempe Lee Fussell

---

1. William White, *Stories For Telling: A Treasury for Christian Storytellers* (Minneapolis, Minn.: Augsburg Press, 1996), pp .122-123.

2. Quoted by C. Douglas Weaver in *A Cloud of Witnesses: Sermon Illustrations and Devotionals from the Christian Heritage* (Macon, Ga.: Smyth & Helwys Pub., 1993), pp. 6-7. From Cyprian, *Treatise* 10.7. in *Ante-Nicene Fathers: Translations of the Writings of the Fathers Down to A. D. 325*, ed. by Alexander Roberts and James Donaldson, Vol. 5 (Grand Rapids, Mich.: W.B. Eerdmans, 1979), p. 286.

Proper 15 • Pentecost 13 • Ordinary Time 20

God Sends Us Ahead

Genesis 45:1-15

This is it. The moment we've all been waiting for. The moment when all the people who thought you'd never amount to anything watch you come out on the stage. The spotlight hits you. The audience stands and the entire hall reverberates with their applause. This is that moment when a man dressed in the finery of the Egyptian court makes himself known to his impoverished brothers. "It's me, Joseph! It's me! Remember me? The brother you threw into a pit? Don't you remember me, Judah? You suggested that you could get some money by selling me into slavery."

At first sight the brothers do not remember. Twenty years made a great difference between the men. Joseph had changed. First he was a slave for a short time in an Egyptian household. Then he spent years in a prison. He no longer had the soft, pampered, playful look of the spoiled boy from Canaan. In addition, Joseph now had the dress and demeanor of a high counselor ("father to the Pharaoh") and kept his distance from those who stood in his audience.

And the brothers had changed also. They had first come to the house of the governor to ask for grain. They had returned because Judah had come to offer himself as a slave in the hope of saving his family. It was Judah who once said, "What profit is it if we slay our brother ... Come, let us sell him to the Ishmaelites" (Genesis 37:26-27). How strange the wheel turns that Judah now offers to give himself as a slave.

As Joseph stands before his brothers, he has them right where we'd love to have all those petty gossipers who have told tales on us. All those obnoxious co-workers who take great joy in criticizing us behind our backs. Joseph has his brothers right where the psalmist would like to put all his malicious witnesses: "At my stumbling they gathered in glee ... slandered me without ceasing ... Let them be put to shame and confusion altogether who rejoice at my calamity!" (Psalm 35:15, 26).

We had a friend who had a good sales position, making almost $50,000 a year. But then the office ran into hard times. Stress mounted and relations between sales representatives and the management broke down. When the office closed down, those who remained refused to give our friend a helpful reference. He was unemployed for two-and-a-half years and never did find a decent job in his profession. He was bitter. He often wished he could bring down those executives who still had cushy jobs but had sent him out without even as much as a good word.

There are some events in our life that make us cringe when we remember them. And there are some people we would love to have at our mercy, as Joseph had his brothers at his mercy. But what did he do at that juncture? He sends all of the Egyptians, all of the witnesses, out of the room. When they are gone, he starts bawling, not crying but bawling. His bawling was so loud they heard his weeping throughout the house and even next door! But his brothers still did not know who he was. Wouldn't you love to know what was going through the brothers' minds when this Egyptian started to break down and cry? Finally, slowly, Joseph regains his composure. He then invites them to come closer, to cross that understood boundary between peasant and ruler. And after exposing his emotions, he says it: "I am your brother, Joseph, whom you sold into Egypt" (Genesis 45:4). Walter Brueggemann, an Old Testament scholar, suggests that the terror and astonishment these brothers experienced would have been similar to the awesome shock the early church experienced in the presence of the risen Christ.[1]

Joseph had his brothers right where he could humiliate them. Right there where he could even the score for the pain and hardship he endured. But instead Joseph comes to his senses. Perhaps for the first time in his life, Joseph realizes that everything his brothers did, every miserable thing that happened to him was twisted by

God into something good. *Because* of his past, God had placed Joseph in a position that enabled him to save a new nation from the ruin of famine. The brothers' actions were God sending him on ahead of them to ensure their future.

Joseph was unable, even with all the power in Egypt, to do anything to change the past. But now he could see that God had been at work redeeming those years. Perhaps Joseph bawled because he was finally released from his captivity of sadness and frustration, and now his brothers were finally freed from their guilt. Joseph basically took a big eraser and wiped off the names of all the people he had blamed for his misfortune. Then in the cleared space he wrote in "Praise only one name, GOD." It was not in a vacuum that Jacob favored Joseph. It wasn't an isolated event that Judah and his brothers sold him into slavery, or that Potiphar's wife sent him off to prison. God chose him. God enslaved him. God imprisoned him. And so to God the praise is given! For it was also God who taught him the way with dreams and God who selected him as counselor to the Pharaoh. Terence Fretheim writes:

> *God has "taken over" what they have done and used it to bring about this end. Their actions have **become** God's by being woven into his life-giving purposes. Even more, **Pharaoh's** actions — elevating Joseph as ruler — have **become** God's!*[2]

We also are unable to change many of the lousy things that happen to us in our lives at the hands of others, but we can allow God to redeem them. All the terrible comments and relationships and events can become God's life-giving purposes. If these incidents have matured us in Christ, if they have made us empathetic and able to help others out of their lethargy, hurt, or bitterness, then our past is redeemed. We have been sent ahead.

Blaming others traps us in the past with them. A black picture of others sticks us with a dim image of God. Charles Stanley writes:

> *There have been times when I felt as if I was on a Ferris wheel. Round and round I would go, experiencing the same*

> *hurt over and over again. "Lord," I would say, "What are you doing? I've already been through this." It was as if He said, "You're right, and when you respond correctly, I'll let you off."*[3]

Joseph is helping his brothers off the Ferris wheel. They are getting off together. They are going as a family into the future that God has planned for them. In his tears, Joseph tells his brothers to come closer. He realizes that he holds no power over them. Just as he realizes his brothers never held any power over him. God was and is the One shaping history, even our history! Augustine concurred with this in a quote from the *Second Helvetic Confession*: "Everything which to vain men seems to happen in nature by accident, occurs only by His Word, because it happens only at His command."

Our friend who was slighted a good reference now works at a local community college. He is out of the cutthroat profession he left and is making use of not only his sales experience but also his math background in his new vocation. I know that he is very good at what he does. And it took all the pressure, rejection, and waiting to get him where he is.

Even if we live through unemployment, or slavery, or imprisonment, or chemotherapy, or whatever, we can claim our life with pride. Paul's words are certainly true: "We know that in all things God works for the good of those who love him."

Tempe Lee Fussell

---

1. Walter Brueggemann, *Genesis: Interpretation — A Bible Commentary for Teaching and Preaching* (Atlanta, Ga.: John Knox Press, 1982), p. 344.

2. Terence E. Fretheim, "The Book of Genesis," in *The New Interpreter's Bible, Volume I* (Nashville, Tenn.: Abingdon Press, 1994), p. 644.

3. Charles Stanley, *How To Handle Adversity* (Nashville, Tenn.: Oliver-Nelson Books, 1989), p. 184.

Proper 16 • *Pentecost 14* • *Ordinary Time 21*

Come Out, Come Out, Wherever You Are!

Exodus 1:8—2:10

Moses was a master of masquerade! He lived a good portion of his life in disguise. From the time he was three months old he went into hiding. At three months he was placed in a basket among the Nile reeds.

The infant princess Elora Danan, in the movie *Willow*, was placed in a basket made of river sticks which quickly became a boat. The little boat was pushed off from the shore seconds before the Queen's death dogs converged on the child's caretaker. Her basket was an escape to a safe land. Moses' basket, though, was no escape boat. He was not meant to escape from Egypt, at least not yet.

Neither was Moses' basket a permanent hiding place. He was placed in the basket to be found at the right time. So he was disguised for that timing. His sister Miriam watched to see who would discover her little brother and when. Moses at three months was disguised as an Egyptian.[1] It was an Egyptian princess, belonging to the house of Pharaoh, who found him. She knew he was a Hebrew infant, but perhaps she accepted him partially because he was disguised as an Egyptian. Every year Egyptians had a festival where they fashioned boxes and baskets and placed likenesses of their gods in these vessels. They were floated down the Nile in a candlelight procession. And there was baby Moses like a little Egyptian god caught up in the reeds.

For all of his youth Moses was disguised as an Egyptian, even while his mother was paid to be his nursemaid. There in Pharaoh's house he lived in the lap of luxury. He enjoyed all the benefits the household of Pharaoh had to offer.

It was as an adult that Moses finally became troubled at living a disguise. His turmoil became public when he saw an Egyptian beating one of his people, and Moses reacted violently. He killed the Egyptian, which meant he had to go into another kind of hiding, hiding as a fugitive, to avoid his own death. His adopted Egyptian grandfather had no mercy for Hebrews, not even one who had been raised as his grandson.

As a fugitive, Moses' masquerade took on another layer. The Hebrew, raised as an Egyptian, now married a Midianite. He hid among the herds and probably learned how to handle and to trade camels. He lived in the house of a priest of yet another religion. There he had a family and named his first son "Alien There." It was perhaps a lonely existence, but Moses was a master of masquerade.

It was there in the hiddenness of being a fugitive that Moses met that other hidden one: the living God. We're told later in the account of Exodus:

> *Moses kept the flock of Jethro his father-in law, the priest of Midian. And he led the flock to the back of the desert, and came to Horeb, the mountain of God. And the angel of the Lord appeared to him as a flame of fire from the midst of a bush. So he looked, and behold, the bush burned with fire, but the bush was not consumed.*
> — Exodus 3:1-2 *(NKJV)*

God, whose name was yet unknown, and thus in some sense was as hidden as Moses who tended Jethro's flocks, appeared in the disguise of a burning bush. The God with no name called out the man's Hebrew name, "Moses, Moses." Even dressed as a Midianite, hidden far out in the wilderness, Moses was found and identified directly by God. Yahweh had flushed Moses out of his hiding for a purpose. God had plans and instructions for this prophet in hiding. The plans and instructions were straightforward: God wanted Moses to stand in public where the Hebrews and Egyptians could see and hear him saying: "I speak for the God of the Hebrews. Let my people go!"

God called Moses, the man of masquerades and hiding, to do something that was completely uncharacteristic for him. That would be like asking the church monotone to be the soloist the first Sunday of every month. Or convincing "Jane," who breaks out in a cold sweat every time she speaks in public, that she needs to start doing the children's sermons every Sunday. Or buying a pretty pink apron for "Don" to persuade him to be the cook at our next church supper, even though he has never touched a pot in his life. There are some things we are not meant to do, and don't want to do!

But there are other things we don't do because we are afraid. I don't accept requests to serve on financial committees because I am afraid my lack of math skills will show up. I've even had nightmares about missing a whole semester of high school math classes, and not realizing my negligence until the day before I had to sit the final exam.

Moses had skipped out on Hebrew classes his whole life. But God now calls him to the powerful court of Pharaoh to speak to him as a Hebrew for the Hebrew people. Harry Emerson Fosdick wrote:

> *Fear imprisons, faith liberates; fear paralyzes, faith empowers; fear disheartens, faith encourages; fear sickens, faith heals; fear makes useless, faith makes serviceable — and most of all, fear puts hopelessness at the heart of life, while faith rejoices in its God.*[2]

Carl Sandburg put years of research into the publication of his volumes on the life of Abraham Lincoln. One reporter asked him, "Mr. Sandburg, what are you going to do now?" His response was, "I think now I'd really like to find out who this fellow Sandburg really is."[3]

God, in the disguise of the burning bush, called Moses to the public court of Pharaoh to be himself. In essence Moses was being told, "You have done enough research on the Egyptian strengths. You have sufficiently studied the dwellers in the wilderness where I will bring my people in the future. It is now time to come out and be one of my own people."

Douglas John Hall has written:

> *The world's suffering is not going to be engaged by people in designer jeans frolicking and posturing in the wilds of Colorado in search of "the meaning of life" (their own!). It will only be met, and transformed, by those who take up the invitation to "come and die."* [4]

Moses had lived the Egyptian life of designer jeans. He had searched for the meaning of his life in the Sinai wilderness. God was now giving him an invitation to come and die for Him.

Ecclesiastes tells us there is a time to be born and a time to die. There is a time to seek and a time to lose. There is a time to be silent and a time to speak. For Moses there had been a time of disguise. God wanted Moses disguised at three months of age to protect him. As an adult, Moses' hiding among the Midianites was effective. But now it was time to stop the masquerade.

There are times when we hide from the hurt that our neighbors are experiencing. There are times when we turn away from the rotten stuff that's going on around us. There are times when we make excuses for not finding and caring for those who have real needs in our community. But life is too short to keep on hiding. It's too short to keep turning away, too short to come up with new excuses. We only have so many years to live to the glory of God. There comes a time to come out of hiding. Dr. Ervin Staub, a teacher at the University of Massachusetts who studies people who reach out and help others who are going through terrible times, says, "One person can greatly influence others by action or passivity" and so it is important to "create a climate where passivity is not okay and where bystanders are also evil."[5]

There's a burning bush out there that's telling us to get over our fears. The flame convicts us to be who God made us to be: to speak up, to reach out, to cry with someone. To be afraid to make a difference for God would be like going through life and never seeing a burning bush. Paul spoke powerfully about how limited our lives are if we hide from God. If we live our life disguised in the flesh and never claim the full, exposed life of God's Spirit, we deny our inheritance, even our identity.

> *If you live according to the flesh you will die, but if by the Spirit you put to death the deeds of the body, you will live. For as many as are led by the Spirit of God, these are the sons of God. For you did not receive the spirit of bondage again to fear, but you received the Spirit of adoption by whom we cry out, "Abba, Father."*
> — Romans 8:13-15 *(NKJV)*

So walk in the light — of a burning bush!

Tempe Lee Fussell

---

1. Martin Buber, *Moses: The Revelation and the Covenant* (New York, N.Y.: Harper & Row, 1946), p. 35, note 35.

2. Quoted in *The Living Pulpit: Faith*, April/June 1992, Vol. 1, No. 2 (Bronx, N.Y.), p. 25.

3. Quoted by Howard W. Roberts, *U-Turns Permitted: God's Grace for Life's Journey* (Louisville, Ken.: Westminster/John Knox Press, 1990), p. 115, note 9.

4. Douglas John Hall, "Suffering: The Badge of Discipline," in *The Living Pulpit: Suffering*, Vol. 4, No. 2, p. 21.

5. Quoted by Sara Nuss-Galles in her article, "Truth Be Told," in *Drew Magazine*, Summer 1997 (Madison, N.J.: Drew University), p. 45.

Proper 17 • Pentecost 15 • Ordinary Time 22

Growing No Feathers

Exodus 3:1-15

When Imelda Marcos was criticized for having 3,000 pairs of shoes in her closet, her excuse was: "Everybody kept their shoes there. The maids ... everybody."[1] When Zsa Zsa Gabor slapped a Beverly Hills policeman, her excuse was: "I am from Hungary. We are descendants of Genghis Khan and Attila the Hun. We are Hungarian freedom fighters."[2] Moses balked when God spoke directly to him, asking him to go liberate a nation of slaves. Moses' excuse was, "I'm not very good with words."

None of these excuses worked. Moses was God's choice even though he was not a natural for the job. He was a Hebrew raised in an Egyptian home and married into a Midianite family. He had, by his own admission, no answers, no authority, no talent for making speeches. Moses wasn't looking for the job. He was drafted. He seemed an unlikely candidate, but he was exactly who God was looking for. It didn't have so much to do with the timing in Moses' life as it had to do with God's timing.

God had reached a point of saturation. God had seen too many stumble under hard loads, had heard too many lashes, God had come to know the daily humiliation of the slaves. The Exodus account tells us of this timing: "And God heard their groaning, and God remembered his covenant with Abraham, with Isaac, and with Jacob. And God saw the people of Israel, and God knew their condition" (Exodus 2:24-25).

God needed someone who was fed up with things as they were and was filled with compassion. Yahweh needed someone who had also seen, heard, and known the life of a Hebrew slave. Every year of Moses' youth he learned about their misery, a misery orchestrated by his own class. And he learned compassion, but his empathy had no outlet. He was Pharaoh's adopted grandson, which made him too close to criticize. With no outlet, one day he exploded! He murdered an Egyptian taskmaster. He killed for a slave. He was so sympathetic, he threw away everything and became an outlaw.

God looks for someone who is filled with the compassion of divine will. In 430 B.C. the historian Thucydides recorded: "It was in those who recovered from the plague that the sick and the dying found the most compassion." Still today, empathy gives zeal. Struggling alcoholics find the strongest motivation from recovering alcoholics. Parents of missing children expend their energy looking for other children who have disappeared. Many respond to the cries they have become accustomed to hearing. Like the man in the city who was walking with a friend on a busy sidewalk and stopped to draw attention to the sound of a cricket. The friend, amazed, wondered how he picked up on that insignificant sound among all the sounds surrounding them. The man responded that you hear what you listen for. To illustrate his point he dropped a coin on the sidewalk. At the sound of that solitary coin everyone all around them stopped and turned in the direction of that sound.[3]

God drafted Moses because Moses heard the cries of the Hebrews. We are reminded by the apostle Paul that "all things work for good for those who love God" (Romans 8:28). Everything that happened to the Hebrews was "recyclable." God could use it for the good. Those who trust just have listen for God's direction.

In our bulletin we have a prayer list. It is not just a checklist for our prayers. It is also fertilizer for our compassion. In our prayers, as we say the words of trust and faith, we also develop our sense of compassion. The deeper we pray for others, the more compassion God has to work with within us. To pray for someone's illness is to have compassion for them as victims. Every scrap of compassion in our lives makes us a possible candidate for the work of God.

But it takes more than compassion. Moses had left Egypt. He had found a way out. He made his way into the Sinai Peninsula into the wilderness land and to the Mountain of Horeb, otherwise known as Mount Sinai. His escape was a dress rehearsal for his people. They, too, would come and camp at this mountain. He was not only filled with compassion for his people, but also he was filled with options. And among these options were God's plans.

Helen Keller has said, "Although the world is full of suffering, it is full also of the overcoming of it." The ones whom God drafts for service are not only full of compassion, they also have the energy of mind and spirit for God to use them. We can excel in compassion, but God passes over us because that's where we stop. We love our church, but hold our breath when something needs doing. We say, "Yes," to helping out with the community center, but we breathe a sigh of relief when we're let off the hook. We wish our children were better educated, but we don't want to make suggestions at the school in case we're volunteered to implement them.

Moses is chosen because he can go back and by returning he can show his people God's way out. When Adolf Hitler rose to power in Germany, a young German theologian, Dietrich Bonhoeffer, came to America to teach and write. He toured and worked in the States until an older theologian, Karl Barth, wrote to him and asked him why he was in America when the German people were suffering. In response Bonhoeffer knew he couldn't avoid the dilemma he thought he had escaped. He went home and joined a plot to assassinate Hitler. Shortly after a failed attempt on Hitler's life, Bonhoeffer was arrested. Only a few days before the conclusion of the war, he was executed. Perhaps it is because he returned home that Bonhoeffer's writings are known around the world. He went back into harm's way, even into death. But in doing so he showed us the way of God.

It is said that some American slaves used an expression when speaking highly of another slave who would not escape and desert his family. It was said he "grew no feathers." Bonhoeffer knew he belonged in Germany. Moses knew that despite his Egyptian upbringing and his Midianite family he was first a Hebrew, and it was time to go home and help his people. Bonhoeffer and Moses "grew no feathers."

And there's a final reason why Moses is the hero of the Exodus. Not only did he have compassion and a plan, he also knew the name of God. Previously, God wasn't known by name, but God told Moses the divine name, "I Am Who I Am." Moses stood in front of a burning bush that did not burn and heard the voice of God: "I Am." He took off his shoes to celebrate the great "I Am." He was told that despite the current suffering of his people that God is "I Am": the One who is present, now, watching, planning, sending, preparing. More important than Moses' past is God's present with him. More pertinent to the Israelites' needs than Moses' background is God's current presence.

"Who are you?" Moses asked. And God answered, "I Am the God of Abraham," not, "I *was* the God of Abraham." God assured Moses, "I *Am* going with you," not, "I *will* meet you there."

To do God's work, God must be persistently present. Our earthly parents send us off to school and pick us up at the end of the day. Our earthly parents care for us until it is time for us to take over and have our own families. But not our heavenly Parent. As draftees into God's service, first and foremost we desire to work *with* God, for our Lord is the great "I Am."

To put ourselves in a position for God to make us useful, we have to keep shedding our shoes. We have to take them off so we can walk in other people's shoes and know how they feel, and what their options are. We have to kick off our shoes every so often to wiggle our toes and touch the holy presence.

We may never see the burning bush, but we can still hear the names that resonate from its flames — the names of those who fill us with compassion. We can hear our name, as one worthy to be used. And we hear God's name, "I Am going with you."

Tempe Lee Fussell

---

1. Leigh W. Rutledge, *Excuses, Excuses* (New York, N.Y.: Penguin Books, 1992), p. 66.

2. *Ibid.*, p. 68.

3. *Synthesis: A Weekly Resource for Preaching and Worship in the Episcopal Tradition* (February 6, 1994), p. 4.

Proper 18 • *Pentecost 16* • *Ordinary Time 23*

Bloody Doorposts

Exodus 12:1-14

When I was about twelve years of age I attended a state Boy Scout jamboree. We camped out in the mountains for an extended weekend. We had to bring food with us to eat, but we were told our Saturday evening meal would be provided. But what we did not know was how it would be provided. About four o'clock in the afternoon we were summoned to the road head. There by the side of the road was a tractor-trailer loaded with live chickens! At our campsite we were divided into groups of three, and from that truck each group, including mine, received a live chicken for the Saturday evening meal.

This was a difficult moment for my fellow scouts and me. We were from the city. We had hardly ever seen a live chicken! Now, we had one in hand and had to kill it to eat supper. We had never killed anything to eat. Chicken legs and thighs had always come to us in plastic packages. Sure, we had caught fish, prepared them and eaten them, but fish weren't like a live chicken walking around pecking at the ground. We took our live chicken back to our campsite. Who was going to kill this chicken? I had heard that my grandmother would wring a chicken's head off, but I didn't know how to do that. Somehow, I don't know how, it fell to me to dispatch this chicken. After building up my courage I took a hatchet in hand. Another boy helped me hold the chicken down, and I chopped off its head. I remember its eyes went blank and then closed. And I remember there was blood — a lot of blood.

One of the most ironic things in life is that for us to live, blood must be spilled. To eat meat means an animal's blood must be poured out. And even if plants don't bleed, they are broken and destroyed by our consumption. Life comes only through death. Something must die for us to live. None of us, of course, think of ourselves as agents of death, and yet every time I sit down to eat a meal, I am aware that something had to die for me to live. This is a profound paradox: I participate in death in order to live. In understanding this basic fact of life, we come to understand a basic fact in the Bible. The two most important meals for people of the Hebrew and Christian Bible are the passover meal in Egypt and the passover meal of the Upper Room. Both events remind us that blood is poured out so we might have life.

In his movie *The Ten Commandments*, Cecil B. DeMille portrays the angel of death that comes on that first Passover night as a greenish, stealthy, creeping mist. Perhaps that is an appropriate image for a harbinger of death. But the word "Passover" to me conveys a stronger image. I see the Lord passing over Egypt in a roar. My image is more like that portrayed in the movie, *Raiders of the Lost Ark*. In that movie when the Ark was opened the angels of death came roaring out with wind and fire, and in a matter of seconds, those who opposed God were dead. This passage in Exodus also speaks of God's swift action: "I will pass through the land of Egypt that night, and I will smite all the first-born in the land of Egypt, both man and beast" (v. 12). Then there is the command to the people to eat the passover meal with "your loins girded, your sandals on your feet, and your staff in your hand; and you shall eat in haste" (v. 11). Everything is portrayed with images of dramatic action; everything is portrayed as decisive. There is no lingering here. No lingering death, no waiting for something to happen. On that night God was on the move in a final, decisive act. God no longer merely sends His messenger Moses; God doesn't remain aloof; God now becomes an actual participant in the release of the Hebrew people. God's patience towards Pharaoh has run out. God now comes to strike Egypt's firstborn. The time for persuasion has ended. God now comes with a roar and in haste.

As a sign of God's decisive action, the people must prepare their meal in a hurry. The bread is unleavened because there is not enough time to allow it to rise. The lamb is not to be dressed, rather the whole carcass is to be cooked intact. Even the cooking is done in the most speedy manner. They are not, of course, to eat it raw, sushi style, but neither can they take the time to heat water and boil the meat. So the people are told to roast the meat over a fire.

All these actions are to be performed in an atmosphere of readiness and urgency. The time is at hand! It's a rush. They're dressed with sandals on and staff in hand, prepared to go at a moment's notice. In other words, what God is about to do is decisive. We have reached the climax of the plagues against Egypt. Death will only pass over the homes with doors painted with blood and will enter at the homes of the rest to strike dead their firstborn. This will be the decisive act. It will release the Hebrew people from slavery into freedom.

But the question arises here: Why must God act in this way? Of particular concern is this verse that says: "The blood shall be a sign for you, upon the houses where you are; and when I see the blood, I will pass over you, and no plague shall fall upon you to destroy you, when I smite the land of Egypt" (Exodus 12:13). But why was blood used as a sign? Why the killing of the firstborn?

It is of course true that God had attempted eleven times with eleven plagues to convince Pharaoh with whom he was dealing. But after eleven impressive and sometimes devastating plagues, Pharaoh still refused to let the Hebrews go. God's grace and forbearance was long and patient with Pharaoh. God had indeed given Pharaoh plenty of opportunities. God gave Pharaoh nearly four times the usual "three times and you're out." God generously granted even more than the usual biblical number of seven. We are right in concluding that Pharaoh was an exceedingly stubborn ruler. And we are also right in understanding that God demonstrated unusual patience.

But still, one cannot help but wonder, after all these signs and wonders, could not one more plague have been used to turn Pharaoh's opinion? After eleven plagues, surely a few more could have been enacted. But no, the generosity of God had run out. The door of opportunity had closed. There was only one plague left: the plague of death, the pouring out of blood.

Here, too, the question arises: Why did the Hebrews have to paint the portals of their doors with blood? Why couldn't they have used another sign? Perhaps a handful of straw hung from the door as a sign that Hebrew slaves dwell here? Perhaps some mortar used to make the bricks smeared around the doors would have announced "Hebrews live here." But no, God demanded blood as a sign that "here in this house live Hebrew slaves." To set the Hebrews free, to release the Hebrews from the hands of Pharaoh, to keep God from striking the firstborn in a Hebrew house, God required death and the pouring out of blood. This is a decisive action. Only through the decisive act of death, the pouring out of blood, can the Hebrews be set free.

This is a difficult concept for us. Our religious faith focuses on giving life. It is a horrendous thing for us to contemplate that God strikes down firstborn children and even innocent dumb animals. But this decisive action impresses on us the extent to which God will go to redeem His people and set them free.

Many years later another firstborn will be born. He will be born in Bethlehem to a woman named Mary, and she will call her firstborn son "Jesus." In the Christian faith he will become the sacrificial lamb for *all* people, not just for the Hebrews, but even for the Egyptians. His blood will be poured out, and because he dies we affirm that God will see his blood and pass over us and give us life.

Perhaps in our more reflective moments we may wonder if the death of Jesus was really necessary for God and for us. But it has been the central message of the Christian faith from its beginning. The apostle Paul made it the center of his preaching, saying, "We preach Christ crucified" (1 Corinthians 1:23); yes, Christ nailed to a cross.

Now it is true that Paul also wrote: "Whatever is true, whatever is honorable, whatever is just, whatever is pure, whatever is lovely, whatever is gracious, if there is any excellence, if there is anything worthy of praise, think about these things" (Philippians 4:8). These are things about life — not death. Paul certainly doesn't say, "Now whatever is bloody, painful, torturous, and deadly, think on these things." And yet, Paul did say, "God shows his love for us in that while we were yet sinners Christ died for us. Since, therefore, we are now justified by his blood, much more shall we be saved by him from the wrath of God" (Romans 5:8-9).

The fact is that in telling the life of Jesus the Gospels devote more than one third of the story to telling about the death of Jesus. Why did the Gospels give so much time and so much length to this subject? The answer comes again from Paul, who writes, "We are justified by (God's) grace as a gift, through the redemption which is in Christ Jesus, whom God put forward as an expiation by his blood ... This was to show God's righteousness, because in his divine forbearance he had passed over former sins" (Romans 3:24-25).

If we study the New Testament, we cannot avoid the subject of the death of Jesus and the subject of his blood poured out. You may well wonder, "Well, why? If God loves us and is Almighty, why couldn't God just speak? Why couldn't God give a command as was done at the creation when God said, 'Let the dry land come forth,' and it did? Why couldn't God just say, 'I forgive you'? Why did Jesus have to shed his blood and die?" This is the same question we ask of that first Passover: "Why couldn't God have spoken directly to Pharaoh and avoided the bloodshed and death?"

The answer in part is found in human relationships. Suppose a husband has been unfaithful to his wife. Being repentant, he goes and tells her how sorry he is and how badly he feels about it. But after hearing his apology, what would it mean if all she says is, "That's okay — it doesn't really matter. It doesn't make any difference — forget it"? Has she enacted forgiveness? NO — what she has said is this: "I don't care enough about you to be bothered by anything you say or do. You're really not that important to me."[1]

What would it take? What would it take really to convince a husband that his wife had forgiven him of unfaithfulness? Just a statement? "Hey, it's okay." No, of course not! What it would take to be convinced of her forgiveness is an act that exhibits reception and forgiveness. Perhaps a reaching out of her hand to hold his hand. Perhaps even a command from her, such as, "Come in here and dry the dishes," would be a way to let him know that his place in the home is restored. Some kind of *action* is necessary to prove acceptance and genuine forgiveness. In a similar manner, an action was necessary from God that God might prove that His acceptance and forgiveness are genuine. As Paul says, "God shows his love for us in that while we were yet sinners Christ died for us" (Romans 5:8). God went the way of death to show us, to prove to us, divine love and forgiveness are genuine.

When the Hebrews lived as slaves to the Egyptians, their only hope for freedom was for God to come and act on their behalf. On that night called Passover, God came in decisive power to show his love for Israel by striking Egypt's firstborn. Since that day the Jewish people have remembered that night with the ritual meal of Passover. We too in the Christian tradition remember the Passover Jesus Christ enacted. There is a direct link between the two events.

In the Christian faith we remember too that God showed His love for us by striking the firstborn of Mary, Jesus the Son of God. We remember God's act of love for us in our celebration of the Eucharist, the memorial meal of Jesus' death. On that night when Jesus celebrated the Passover meal with his disciples, we are told that after he had given thanks, he took the cup and said, "This cup is the new covenant in my blood" (1 Corinthians 11:25). And when we reenact this meal and pass the cup to one another, we say, "This is the blood of Christ shed for you."

Few of us probably give much thought to what we are doing when we receive the cup of the new covenant in Jesus' blood. Drinking the blood of Jesus Christ? In the synagogue in Capernaum, Jesus taught, "Truly, truly, I say to you, unless you eat the flesh of the Son of man and drink his blood, you have no life in you; he who eats my flesh and drinks my blood has eternal life, and I will raise him up at the last day. For my flesh is food indeed, and my blood is drink indeed" (John 6:53-55). As a result, many who followed Jesus said his words were too hard to understand. From that time on we're told, "Many of his disciples drew back and no longer went about with him" (John 6:66).

The thought of a meal with juice symbolizing blood is awesome and barbaric to the outsider. But in the drinking of that cup we spread the blood of Jesus Christ on the doorposts of our lives. We do it in the belief and out of the assurance that God acts decisively for us in Jesus Christ as He did for the Hebrews on that

Passover night. God has not hesitated. God has not waited for us to change our minds. No, God comes and acts decisively to set us free.

Curtis Fussell

---

1. Shirley Guthrie, *Christian Doctrine*, rev. ed. (Louisville, Ken.: Westminster/John Knox Press, 1994), p. 260.

Proper 19 • *Pentecost 17* • *Ordinary Time 24*

Going Through The Waters

Exodus 14:19-31

I suppose when we hear this passage about the parting of the Reed Sea, many of us cannot help but recall that scene in the movie *The Ten Commandments*. There is Moses, played by Charlton Heston, in a flowing black robe, long hair blowing in the wind, and his arms lifted up with one hand holding the staff that God had given him. The sea suddenly heaves and parts, creating a path with rolling walls of water on either side. Then, Israel marches through on dry land, barely ahead of the pursuing Egyptian army.

I understand that nowadays a lot of people see this scene reenacted several times a day at Universal Studios in Hollywood. It could well be that more people know about this scene from Hollywood than they do from the Bible. But it's not surprising that Hollywood has made use of this dramatic Biblical event. It speaks to us on many levels: escape to freedom, miracle of God, water that saves the good guys and destroys the bad guys.

Biblical scholars have attempted to explain the crossing of the Reed Sea as a natural event. They point out that in that region the area is flat and marshy and occasionally covered by shallow water driven in at high tide by the wind. When it is covered by water, this same wind can blow in, push the water aside, and open a path. While plausible, such an explanation has no Hollywood technicolor. Besides, that the wind blew on that particular day, and at that particular hour, when the Israelites needed to cross, certainly points to something miraculous. But this passage doesn't want us to ponder the parting of waters; rather, it wants to tell us something more wondrous. Namely, that God is at work here. The only true explanation for what took place is the presence and power of God, who brings life and overcomes evil, leading His people to a new way of life. The really profound miracle here in crossing the Reed Sea is God's faithfulness to Israel. How it all happened is another question, but *who* made it happen is what the Exodus is all about. Crossing the Reed Sea is a witness to God and one that calls us to faith.

Here we have Israel, almost lost and forgotten in the world. As the expression goes, "How odd of God to choose the Jews." They had become slaves in Egypt — nobodies with no status, or nation, or power. All they had was the memory of a promise to Abraham that his descendants would become a great nation, from a God whose name they could not even remember. Yet this God, Yahweh, remembered. Yahweh remembered His people and His promise. The time had now come for God to fulfill His promise, to set the descendants of Abraham free, and establish them as a people with respect and honor for His name. God, who remembers His promise and acts to make it real, explains this passage.

Knowing this witness to God and this calling to faith, the Christian church has also made use of this scene as readily as Hollywood. Crossing through the waters of the Reed Sea, leaving behind an old way of life and embarking on the other side to a new way of life, cannot help but remind us of water baptism. It reminds us that God is the One who is graciously at work in our lives, the One who makes it possible to be rescued and gives us life, new and fresh.

In the Christian faith the act of going through the baptismal waters proclaims and gives witness to the gracious presence and work of God. In the baptism of our members, we remember the crossing of the Reed Sea. Our baptism points to God's act of setting us free from our slavery to sin, crossing over to a new life, the old enemies destroyed.

When Jesus met his disciples for the last time, the Gospel of Matthew tells us that the last words he spoke to them were, "Go and make disciples ... baptizing them" (Matthew 28:19). Ever since that time, going through the waters has meant freedom, newness of life, the past left behind, a new future straight ahead. Going through the waters has not meant something we dreamed up, or something we achieved. No, it has meant only this: the power of God's presence and redeeming work to give us life.

To witness clearly to our new lives we distinctly baptize "in the name of the Father, the Son, and the Holy Spirit." Never in the name of Paul, or Apollos, or Peter, or the name of some dearly beloved preacher. No, we go through the waters, we baptize, in the name of God, to bear witness to God and the call for faith in God.

And so in baptism we are given God's name to live by. God's name gives us an identity; it declares that we are somebody. Just as the Israelites were nobodies before going through the water, before our baptism we were nobody. But after going through the water, God made us somebody. This is what we testify. God made us; God led us through to new life.

A man describes how one day he said to his mother that one of the most useful courses he took in high school was typing. Everyday he is grateful that he knows how to type. Typing is a skill he uses nearly everyday of his life.

In response to that comment his mother responded, "Aren't you glad I made you take typing?" And he said, "You made me take typing? I don't remember you making me take typing." She said, "Oh, yes, I remember you saying that you didn't think you needed to learn to type. You thought it would be a waste of time. But I told you that you needed to know how to type so you wouldn't have to depend on someone else to do your typing. You hated it at first, but I made you stick with it."

There he was congratulating himself on his own wisdom and foresight in deciding to learn typing, only to be reminded that it was not his idea at all. In fact, he had little to congratulate himself for. His typing skill is a gifted power. It was the power of someone else's care and direction that has provided him this useful and valuable skill.[1]

The same is true of our presence here in the church. We often congratulate ourselves for being here, but the truth is, someone else cared enough about us to direct us here. We might think we get up out of our own decision to be here, but chances are it is a habit that was instilled in you by someone else. And I would add that it is definitely the Spirit that keeps us coming. In our baptism we profess our relationship to God, but we cannot take the credit. We have been claimed by God. We cannot take the glory for our inheritance.

Normally, our lives are not nearly so dramatic as crossing the Reed Sea. For the most part we come to church to learn about God, to speak to God, to get spiritual support to make it through a typical week, to receive insights on how to live in the image and grace of Jesus Christ. As the bumper sticker says, "Rough week at work? See me in church." Indeed, I agree wholeheartedly.

But what about those big, earth-shaking, fundamental human situations we sometimes find ourselves in that can't be solved by anything we say or do? What then? Here at worship is the court of last appeal, because all other avenues are exhausted. Here we identify with Jesus on the cross when he cries out, "My God, my God, why have you forsaken me?" (Mark 15:34).

The doctor comes and tells you the illness is terminal; there's no cure. You receive word that the company you work for is closing. Everything you worked for, your home, and your dreams are pulled out from under your feet. You are betrayed by someone you trusted. You watch the evening news of starving children, poverty, and civil wars. The earth shakes and you are powerless to stop it, powerless to right the wrong.

In crossing the Reed Sea we are reminded that in every life dark forces threaten to overtake us. But in going through the waters we are also reminded that finally our lives are in the hands of God. When the stars fall and the sea roars — and everything comes loose — what then? Only the tenacity of faith and hope.

Jesus says, "Raise your heads, because your redemption is drawing near" (Luke 21:28). Salvation isn't coming because we're optimistic, or because we work our way out of it, or think positively about it. Salvation comes because God acts, because God does something, because God leads us through. The Christian hope is set on what God will do when we can do nothing. God gives us the victory when we are utterly defeated.

In 1525, Martin Luther was besieged with threats and surrounded by enemies on all sides. He was excommunicated from the Roman Church. Utter despair and discouragement infected him. His friends tried to get him out of his depression, but couldn't. One day he came home and found his wife Catherine wearing a funeral dress and weeping in grief. Luther asked her, "Catherine, who died?" She said, "God is dead, and I can't bear it; all his work is overthrown." Luther was shocked at hearing what could only be described as blasphemy from his wife's mouth. To which Catherine responded, "Well, you've been going around acting as if God were dead, as if God no longer was here to keep us. So I thought I should join the funeral and your bereavement."[2]

Catherine's remark struck home. Luther realized he had taken his eyes off the Redeemer. He had to be reminded that it is God who gives the victory. To be reminded that the future belongs to God. It is a gift given to us to the glory of God.

When we were baptized, when the water was parted and splashed on our heads, we were given a name and told we are somebody. It was a gift; the past was put behind us; all our excuses were washed away; we were given a future.

What kind of future? A totally new and different future. One that embraces life in new and startling ways. I am reminded of what this future looks like from a story Fred Craddock told that he said is found in Jewish writings. The story is that one day the Almighty heard some angels whooping and hollering, squealing with delight. The Almighty asked, "What's all the excitement about?" And the angels said, "We got 'em, Lord. We got 'em. When the water tumbled in, we got those Egyptians!" And the Almighty said, "You are dismissed from my house. For you have not seen that the Egyptians are also my children."[3]

When the water was parted and ran down our foreheads, we were declared to be free people. It was a gift and a great honor, but also a great responsibility. It is our responsibility to share the joy and grace of God to the world, to speak words of encouragement to others, to show compassion and mercy, to have patience and love towards others. These are not easy things to do by any means, and our past failures in these matters haunt us.

But the question is: What will we do now? We have received this gift: the water of baptism and the Spirit. Jesus took this gift and lived the good news, rejoicing in and sharing the grace of God. What will we do now? We have the gift — the gift of God's power and presence in our lives. May we rejoice in it and share it.

Curtis Fussell

---

1. Adapted from William Willimon's sermon, "The Gifted," in *Pulpit Resource* Vol. 23, No. 1 (Logos Productions: Inver Grove Heights, Minn.), p. 10.

2. Adapted from C. Douglas Weaver, *A Cloud of Witnesses: Sermon Illustrations and Devotionals from the Christian Heritage* (Macon, Ga.: Smyth & Helwys, 1993), p. 73.

3. Source unknown.

Proper 20 • *Pentecost 18* • *Ordinary Time 25*

The Rain Of Bread

Exodus 16:2-15

There is nothing like heading out into the back country, carrying on your back everything you need to survive. Enjoying nature, listening only to the sounds of wildlife, having a bit of creation all to yourself. Of course, there is one downside to it all — the food. Cans are out of the question, they're too heavy to carry. That leaves only the packaged, freezed-dried variety of food. The pictures on the outside of these packages look inviting, but the actual stuff is all texture and no taste. If there's one complaint heard again and again during a wilderness experience, it's the food.

This is what we find Israel doing. Here they are in the wilderness, and they are complaining about the food. They complain to Moses, "Better to have stayed in Egypt as slaves where we had food to eat, than to live here as starving free people." Immediately, it is God, not Moses, who responds to the cry of the people, saying, "I am going to rain bread from heaven for you, and each day you will have enough." Israel is to learn once more that it is God who rescues them. In the wilderness of life, it is God who provides and rescues, and none other. In the wilderness of life, there is not emptiness; rather, God is present to sustain and provide.

Then it happened. A flock of quail descended on the camp. Then something extraordinary was sent to them. In the morning they found the ground covered with a fine, flaky substance. When gathered it could be prepared and eaten like bread. On first seeing this bread the people asked, "What is it?" This question in Hebrew is "man hu," or "manna," the bread from heaven. It had to be gathered on a daily basis. It wouldn't keep overnight. It would go bad, unfit to eat, like leftover french fries. You couldn't store it and eat it the next day. You could only gather as much as you could eat that day. No doubt this is part of the origin of the prayer, "Give us this day our daily bread." Daily it rained bread from heaven. And daily the people were reminded that in the wilderness of life, God is present to sustain and provide for them. And so they lived by the providence of God, one day at a time.

We are not to think that quail and manna were the only food the Israelites had to eat, because we are told they brought flocks and herds with them out of Egypt. Plus, they would have been able to find other food in the canyons and oases they visited. But this manna was a staple food that they ate for forty years, and it became a symbol of God's providence in the wilderness of life. Perhaps like Bubba in the movie *Forrest Gump*, who recited for two days all the different ways you can eat shrimp, the Israelites must have had raw manna, baked manna, fried manna, boiled manna, and manna any way you like it. But this daily manna became a symbol for Israel of God's daily care for them during their wilderness journey. In Psalm 78 it was remembered as God's gracious act for them in spite of their unfaithfulness: "They tested God in their heart by demanding the food they craved ... Therefore, the Lord was full of wrath ... Yet he rained down upon them manna to eat, and gave them the grain of heaven" (Psalm 78:18, 21, 24).

Since the time before Jesus, this bread the Israelites ate has been known to be a sap that is sucked from a bush by an insect. These insects then excrete the excess sap as a small, yellow-white flake that is rich in carbohydrates and sugars. In many ways this desert insect is like a honeybee who takes up nectar from flowers and regurgitates it as honey. However, manna flakes quickly dry up and spoil in the desert heat, so a daily portion is all anyone can gather. The Bedouin people who live in that region today still collect these flakes and make them into a bread. And they also call this bread "manna."

Barbara Taylor, an Episcopal priest in Georgia, describes how growing up in the South she ate grits without knowing what they were. Finally, one day when she was twelve years of age, she asked a friend if he knew where grits came from. He said, "The truth?"

She said, "Yes, of course." And he said, grinning wickedly, "Grits come from small bugs that live in colonies on the surface of freshwater lakes, like algae, and at the end of every summer they're harvested, shelled, and dried in the sun so you can't ever tell they had legs. Mmmm. Tasty bugs."[1]

The Israelites who wandered in the wilderness may have known perfectly well about the natural source of the manna. But whether they did or did not, they recognized that God had provided for them. It was not merely a natural phenomena; it was recognized as God's act of grace. It is like the story of a man who entered a monastic order. When he sat down to his first meal, the bread was served and he found it was delicious. The man turned to one of the monks and asked, "Did we make this bread or was it given to us?" And the monk replied, "Yes!" Well, which is it? And the answer is this: Life is both given to us and created by us.[2]

Perhaps you are familiar with the cartoon *Kudzu*. It's a cartoon about a preacher by the name of Rev. Will B. Dunn, who looks rather goofy, wears a wide-brim black hat, but who tries hard to provide ministry to people who are silly and self-serving. In one of the *Kudzu* cartoons Rev. Will B. Dunn is shown reading from the pulpit Bible the Lord's Prayer: "Give us this day our daily ... low-fat, low-cholesterol, salt-free bread." The last frame has Rev. Dunn saying to himself, "I hate these modern translations."[3]

You see, Rev. Will B. Dunn knows that the Lord's Prayer is a prayer for daily bread and the physical ability to acquire it. But he also knows this prayer is more than about bread itself. To ask God to give us this day our daily bread is to ask not only for physical food, but also spiritual food. Yes, in the Lord's Prayer we are asking for bread we can slice and make into sandwiches, but in that prayer we are also asking for the bread of life: Jesus Christ.

No matter who we are, no matter how sophisticated, talented, or intelligent we may be, we all need to eat to survive. We need physical nourishment. And no matter how sophisticated, talented, or intelligent we may be, we also need spiritual food to survive. We need spiritual nourishment. As Jesus put it so eloquently, "We do not live by bread alone, but by every word that comes from the mouth of God" (Matthew 4:4).

The Hebrew people have arrived in the desert wilderness. There is not enough food for them to eat. They long for the food they remember being readily available in Egypt. They want bread; they want the bread of life. We too have come here with this same desire. We have all come here wanting the bread of life in one way or another. Some of us want an answer about the direction of our lives. So we ask, "Lord, show us the way forward." Some of us want healing. So we ask, "Lord, give us healing; touch me; make me whole." Some of us want a change in life. "Lord, make me new; renew my life." We have come here seeking life, wanting to be nourished, to have peace of mind, to be successful, to be loved; all because we are hungry.

But part of satisfying this hunger is not only telling God what we want, but also asking, "Lord, what do you want from me?" So often we say to ourselves, "If I just reach this point, if I just get this, everything will be all right." But will it? Hasn't it been your experience that when you get a new car, a new house, a new job it's enjoyable for a while, but it doesn't really satisfy you? It doesn't satisfy your hunger. You still find yourself longing for something else, thinking *that* will satisfy your hunger. Saint Augustine spoke to this hunger, saying, "Our souls are not satisfied until they find rest in God." Is it too much to suggest that we trust our lives to God, that God will provide and satisfy our deepest hungers? What does God want from us? God wants our trust that our heavenly Lord will provide for us and satisfy our deepest hungers.

John Killinger tells a story I think will help us to understand what it means to trust God, knowing that God is present to satisfy our deepest hungers. It is the story of a man who came to faith in God after years of merely believing in God. The man has a daughter who had become an alcoholic when she was in junior high school, and began taking hard drugs by the time she reached high school. He described how he had placed her in expensive drug treatment centers three times, but each time when she was released, she had gone back on drugs.

Before she graduated from high school she left home and went to a big city, where she hit rock bottom. Before long she was arrested and received a six-month prison sentence. After she had spent a few days in jail, the father said, "She called me and pleaded with me to sign a release for her. But after following the advice of an Al-Anon group, I refused to sign the release. It was the hardest thing I had ever done. A month later, I telephoned her and asked her if she wanted to come home. She said yes, and I drove to the jail to pick her up. She was so thin, she didn't even look like my daughter."

At the end of telling this story, the man spoke of how God had sustained him through this entire ordeal, and still was sustaining him as the ordeal continued. He said, "Before, I believed in God. But now I have faith. I could not have gotten through without God."[4]

When God sent the manna it was meant to satisfy the physical hunger of the people, but above all it was meant to satisfy their spiritual hunger, that they should "know that I am the Lord your God" (v. 12).

Is it too much to suggest that we trust our lives to God, that God will provide and satisfy our deepest hungers? The first few sentences of the Serenity Prayer are known perhaps by all of us. It says, "God grant me the serenity to accept the things I cannot change; the courage to change the things I can; and the wisdom to know the difference."

What is not well known, however, are the last sentences of this prayer. And yet these words speak to the profound trust we have in God to give us what we need in those times of deep hunger. "Help me, O God, to live one day at a time, enjoying one minute at a time, accepting hardship as the pathway to peace, taking as you did this sinful world as it is, not as it would be, trusting that you will make all things right, if I surrender to your will. So that I may be reasonably happy in this life, and supremely happy with you forever in the next life."

On that day the manna from heaven was collected and made into bread, and was eaten, the people of Israel knew it was from the Lord their God. And they never forgot who gave them the bread of life, who gave them life itself. May we also never forget to trust that God will provide for us and satisfy our deepest hungers.

Curtis Fussell

1. Adapted from Barbara Taylor's sermon, "Bread of Angels," in *Bread of Angels* (Boston, Mass.: Cowley Publications, 1997), p. 8.

2. From Fred Craddock's sermon, "Preaching Stories of Jesus," in *Lectionary Homiletics*, Vol. VII, No. 7, June 1996 (Midlothian, Va.), pp. 2, 10.

3. Cited in the journal *Homiletics*, July/September 1997, Vol. 9, No. 3 (Canton, Oh.: Communication Resources, Inc.), p. 30.

4. John Killinger, *The Greatest Teachings of Jesus* (Nashville, Tenn.: Abingdon Press, 1993), p. 29.

Proper 21 • *Pentecost 19* • *Ordinary Time 26*

It's Not Over When The Fat Lady Sings

Exodus 17:1-7

Consider this list: a local restaurant under construction, a high school dropout, the cross-stitch I've been working on for six years, a young person killed in an accident. All of these have one thing in common: they describe something that has gone unfinished. A building, an education, a craft, a life. There are thousands of things and thousands of people around us that go unfinished. Some people start something and stop because they can't take criticism. Others stop because they're content with what they've done to that point. Still others have their life taken tragically from them, unfinished. What can we say about the unfinished business of life? I myself have been drawn to that expression that says, "Some look at the glass and say, 'It's half empty.' Others look at the glass and say, 'It's half full.' I look at the glass and say, 'It's too big!'"

Life has so many options, and is so big, we're constantly faced with being unfinished. One excuse we often hear expressed is: "Be patient with me; God isn't finished with me yet!" Only God has the luxury of time, patience, and power. From the beginning God has seen things through to the end. God didn't make us until God had already created everything that would sustain us. And God didn't rest on the seventh day until the work of creation was finished. Yahweh promised Abraham millions of descendants, and chose Joshua to take them to their own land. And God didn't tell Jeremiah to prophesy the fall of Jerusalem without knowing that Haggai would be commissioned to lead the remnant in rebuilding the city. God didn't choose the seed of David without knowing that Jesus of Nazareth would finish that divinely-initiated line.

But in every generation we think God is like us. We get anxious that God will walk away from us because God is bored or the divine feelings have been hurt. The Hebrew people yell at Moses, "You and God brought us out to the desert. Now are you going to let us die?" It's the third time that the people panicked. In just a few months the Hebrews have questioned Moses' authority again and again. "Doesn't God supply you with power? Why did you save us just to kill us in the wilderness?"

Finally, on this occasion their panic infects Moses. There's an ancient Hungarian proverb that says: "If someone calls you a horse, laugh at him. If a second person calls you a horse, think about it. If a third person calls you a horse, maybe you should go buy a saddle."

This is the third occasion when the people doubted whether Moses had any pull with God. Martin Buber reminds us that the semi-nomadic Israelites had the wrong idea. They believed that only if things were going well for them did their leader have divine authority. And because life's necessities were in very short supply, evidently there was a rift between Moses and God.[1]

After hearing this three times, Moses buys the saddle. He panics too! "God, did you put me through all that trouble with Pharaoh just to have my people bring me out into the desert and stone me?" He sounds like Oral Roberts, who panicked and told his television audience, "If I don't raise eight million dollars, God won't let me live!" Moses is so panicked that God has to lead him through the miracle, step by step, like a distraught caller making a 911 call. God responds almost condescendingly. "It's okay, Moses. Take a few deep breaths. Now, I want you to go stand before the people. You can do it. You've done it many times before. When you go before the people take some elders with you. Are you with me? Now this is very important: Take with you the rod I gave you, that you used to separate the Sea." God has to walk Moses through his panic because Moses is so paralyzed by the skepticism of the people.

There is something sorely missing in the Sinai Desert: it's trust. Look in the dictionary for the word "faith." The primary definition for faith is reliance or trust. Insecurity cannot breed faith anymore than hunger can breed happiness. We find then that God brings water out of the rock, not merely to satisfy a thirsty people, but to build trust in a community that had forgotten how to rely on anyone except slave masters. They needed to live free and open lives. They had to rediscover how to trust God.

There is no way to live a faithful life without trusting that we are still part of God's salvation story. It's like the two brothers who got caught in floodwaters. The two brothers were separated by a swift current but were only yards apart. The brother on the safe side of the current yelled, "Swim hard; I'll grab you!" But the brother who was in danger wasn't willing to trust his brother's grasp. So instead of swimming hard, he grabbed a branch wedged in some rocks and worked his way through the current, hand over hand. Halfway through the current, the branch broke free from its anchor and followed the current, taking the boy with it. The brother on the safe side tried to grab him, but the branch knocked him in the chest and pushed him back.

We can rely on things that look secure. We can rely on people who appear strong. But unless we trust in God, everything we have lived for will be swept away.

I don't want to die yet. And if I live to be a healthy eighty years old, I'll still feel the same way. Indeed, I look forward to heaven, but there is so much in the world to see and do and enjoy. They say more and more people are living to be over one hundred years of age. The Delany sisters, at the ages of 103 and 105, still believe they are learning new things every day. Because of their age they have become celebrities, with several books, television appearances, and even a modeling contract! Bessie Delany acknowledges that even if you live to be over 100 you don't exhaust life. She stated, "Heaven is my home, but, honey, I ain't homesick yet!"[2]

Even if I were to live to be over one hundred, I know my life would still end unfinished. Even if by some twist of aging, I should develop into an efficient, highly organized, goal-oriented perfectionist, there's going to be some loose ends at the end of my life. I will still need to seek forgiveness; there will still be wonders to discover and truths to illuminate my life. Even if I grow to be ancient and mature, my life will not be complete. My life has no conclusion until it becomes part of God's salvation story. God alone is our Alpha and Omega.

Paul passed on this brand of trust when he wrote: "I am sure that He who began a good work in you will bring it to completion at the day of Jesus Christ" (Philippians 1:6). If God is going to finish up what we're doing, then God expects us to use our lives to get it off to a good start. You've heard the expression, "It's not over until the fat lady sings." But we hold out for something far more climactic. It is not over until "God's will be done, on earth as it is in heaven. Amen." The Amen here at the end does not mean "the end," it means "it will be done," or better, "God finish it."

Tempe Lee Fussell

---

1. Martin Buber, *Moses: The Revelation and the Covenant* (New York, N.Y.: Harper & Row, 1946), p. 88.

2. Sarah and Elizabeth Delany with Amy Hill Hearth, *The Delany Sisters' Book of Everyday Wisdom*, read by Iona Morris, Audio Renaissance Tapes: Library Edition (Los Angeles, Calif.: Cassette Productions Unlimited, 1994), tape 2, side 4.

Lectionary Preaching After Pentecost

The following index will aid the user of this book in matching the correct Sunday with the appropriate text during Pentecost. All texts in this book are from the series for Lesson One, Revised Common Lectionary. (Note that the ELCA division of Lutheranism is now following the Revised Common Lectionary.) The Lutheran and Roman Catholic designations indicate days comparable to Sundays on which Revised Common Lectionary Propers are used.

(Fixed dates do not pertain to Lutheran Lectionary)

Fixed Date Lectionaries *Revised Common (including ELCA)* *and Roman Catholic*	Lutheran Lectionary *Lutheran*
The Day of Pentecost	The Day of Pentecost
The Holy Trinity	The Holy Trinity
May 29-June 4 — Proper 4, Ordinary Time 9	Pentecost 2
June 5-11 — Proper 5, Ordinary Time 10	Pentecost 3
June 12-18 — Proper 6, Ordinary Time 11	Pentecost 4
June 19-25 — Proper 7, Ordinary Time 12	Pentecost 5
June 26-July 2 — Proper 8, Ordinary Time 13	Pentecost 6
July 3-9 — Proper 9, Ordinary Time 14	Pentecost 7
July 10-16 — Proper 10, Ordinary Time 15	Pentecost 8
July 17-23 — Proper 11, Ordinary Time 16	Pentecost 9
July 24-30 — Proper 12, Ordinary Time 17	Pentecost 10
July 31-Aug. 6 — Proper 13, Ordinary Time 18	Pentecost 11
Aug. 7-13 — Proper 14, Ordinary Time 19	Pentecost 12
Aug. 14-20 — Proper 15, Ordinary Time 20	Pentecost 13
Aug. 21-27 — Proper 16, Ordinary Time 21	Pentecost 14
Aug. 28-Sept. 3 — Proper 17, Ordinary Time 22	Pentecost 15
Sept. 4-10 — Proper 18, Ordinary Time 23	Pentecost 16
Sept. 11-17 — Proper 19, Ordinary Time 24	Pentecost 17
Sept. 18-24 — Proper 20, Ordinary Time 25	Pentecost 18

Sept. 25-Oct. 1 — Proper 21, Ordinary Time 26	Pentecost 19
Oct. 2-8 — Proper 22, Ordinary Time 27	Pentecost 20
Oct. 9-15 — Proper 23, Ordinary Time 28	Pentecost 21
Oct. 16-22 — Proper 24, Ordinary Time 29	Pentecost 22
Oct. 23-29 — Proper 25, Ordinary Time 30	Pentecost 23
Oct. 30-Nov. 5 — Proper 26, Ordinary Time 31	Pentecost 24
Nov. 6-12 — Proper 27, Ordinary Time 32	Pentecost 25
Nov. 13-19 — Proper 28, Ordinary Time 33	Pentecost 26
	Pentecost 27
Nov. 20-26 — Christ the King	Christ the King

Reformation Day (or last Sunday in October) is October 31 (Revised Common, Lutheran)

All Saints' Day (or first Sunday in November) is November 1 (Revised Common, Lutheran, Roman Catholic)

Books In This Cycle A Series

GOSPEL SET
And Then Came The Angel
Sermons for Advent/Christmas/Epiphany
William B. Kincaid, III

The Lord Is Risen! He Is Risen Indeed! He Really Is!
Sermons For Lent/Easter
Richard L. Sheffield

No Post-Easter Slump
Sermons For Sundays After Pentecost (First Third)
Wayne H. Keller

We Walk By Faith
Sermons For Sundays After Pentecost (Middle Third)
Richard Gribble

Where Gratitude Abounds
Sermons For Sundays After Pentecost (Last Third)
Joseph M. Freeman

FIRST LESSON SET
Between Gloom And Glory
Sermons For Advent/Christmas/Epiphany
R. Glen Miles

Cross, Resurrection, And Ascension
Sermons For Lent/Easter
Richard Gribble

Is Anything Too Wonderful For The Lord?
Sermons For Sundays After Pentecost (First Third)
Leonard W. Mann

The Divine Salvage
Sermons For Sundays After Pentecost (Middle Third)
R. Curtis and Tempe Fussell

When God Says, "Let Me Alone"
Sermons For Sundays After Pentecost (Last Third)
William A. Jones

SECOND LESSON SET
Moving At The Speed Of Light
Sermons For Advent/Christmas/Epiphany
Frank Luchsinger

Love Is Your Disguise
Sermons For Lent/Easter
Frank Luchsinger

www.ingramcontent.com/pod-product-compliance
Lightning Source LLC
Chambersburg PA
CBHW072015060426
42446CB00043B/2554